TIERS OF HEALING I

Self Guided Workbook...Journey Through Grief

by

ANNE BROWNING

TIERS OF HEALING
OVERVIEW & WELCOME

Welcome to *Tiers of Healing*. Let us assure you, we have been right where you are. Each of us has suffered great loss, grieved, and thought life would never be good again. Life *will* be good again. If we were able to move from a place of hopelessness and despair to a place where there was a glimmer of hope, we know you will be able to do the same. If we were able to build on that hope and find a grudging sense of acceptance for all that was lost to us, we know that you will also be able to do the same. If each of us was able to find a new vision for what would one day become our new normal, we are certain it is possible for you. Finally, if we, with little support, were able to take the steps to reach that vision and live a full and joyful life, we know you will have the capability to take those steps. We are here to support you.

Originally, *Tiers of Healing* was designed to be facilitated in small groups, and in fact, there are groups that meet to move through all the Tiers of Loss, finding hope and friendship along the way. What you have purchased has many of the components from our group program but is designed for individual study. We urge you to find someone to share your journey with, perhaps a trusted friend, mentor, or coach. We welcome you to share with us at anne@tiersofhealing.com.

To make the most of this material, give yourself the gift of time. Healing loss is possible if you do the work that is required. The amount of time will vary with each individual: a maximum of three hours a day and minimum of forty minutes is a good place to begin. Know you are not alone. The exercises in these workbooks are not difficult, yet they can be profound and must be assimilated before moving forward.

Find a quiet place and consecrate it for your healing. Bless the space, perhaps adding flowers or meaningful mementos. You will need a place to write as well as writing materials. Some exercises use crayons or modeling clay. Please note the supplies needed at the start of each session.

Each session takes approximately ten to fifteen minutes to read (some longer) and fifteen to thirty minutes to complete the exercises. All sessions include a music suggestion. You may use the suggestion provided or find your own music, but we strongly urge you to include music in your healing journey.

We have included a "Weather Report Chart." This is important—copy it and keep it in a place where you can make daily notes. Often during times of loss and chaos, we feel as if we are making no progress. The weather report is an excellent tool to note those days that were sunny and to also aide you in noting what it was you did or what you were thinking that helped make the day sunny. Equally, it can be a great way to recognize patterns and trends in your behavior—perhaps if you find yourself getting worse day after day, week after week. We urge you to care for yourself and seek professional help in addition to this self-help guide. It may take a village to raise a child, but it takes an army to heal a loss.

We celebrate your courage. Loss must be healed. It has a way of hiding deep within the soul, robbing us of energy, joy, and motivation. Often, we may believe we have "gotten past it," yet may notice that we are easily angered, tire more quickly, or just see the world as a place of dreary sameness. Once the hurt is healed, the joy in living returns and life once again becomes hopeful.

At no time do we tell you that loss is not painful. It is. At no time do we tell you that you will stop the missing. You won't. At no time do we tell you that life will be like it used to be. It won't. What we do tell you is that although pain comes to us all, misery is a choice, and you *can* choose something else. What we do tell you is that there is always something to miss as you grow, yet there can be smiles, laughter, and joyful memories rather than longing. Finally, we tell you that you do not know what lies ahead. Your life has changed. There will be more joy, laughter, and love. Of course, it will be different than it was, but it will be your new normal and you may even like it. There is at least hope that you will one day be on the other side of your loss and you will be OK. We know, we have traveled the path, and we are OK. Most days, we are better than OK.

Welcome. We are here for you and with you.

Contact info:

anne@tiersofhealing.com

ACKNOWLEDGMENTS

Tiers of Healing Self Study Guides are based on a program Linda Debelser Owen and I created. The four-part program is designed for small groups. Tiers of Healing for groups, was and continues to be, a mission of love for both Linda and myself. I owe a deep thanks to Linda for her vision, her dedication, and most importantly, her friendship.

There were months and months of talks, writing, rewriting, editing and more editing and rewriting. Not once did I hear Linda complain about the work involved. She kept her eye on her vision of reaching hurting people and helping them heal. Linda lives in Canada and runs the Canadian Tiers program. She has delivered the group material to churches, women fighting breast cancer, indigenous people who are still recovering from land loss and she is the woman I turn to when I need a laugh, a push or a strong shoulder. She is my hero. I acknowledge her expertise, her commitment, her integrity and her love.

I want to acknowledge all the men, women and children who have had a loss and continue to live their lives fully and who have the compassion to reach out to others who are in pain. I acknowledge those to whom this book is dedicated, individuals who are in pain and feel alone. I assure you, you are not alone.

We are here and we have known your pain.

Donna Lipman of Austin Texas is the woman who recorded the DVD portion of the Tiers of Healing for Groups. She is a woman of deep compassion, brilliant insights. Her commitment to filling our world with peace and joy was begun at birth. Everyone adores Donna. She has delivered the Tiers for Groups in Austin and she used the material in a very real way when her husband, Terry Lipman, who did the filming for the DVD, died suddenly. I acknowledge her, love her and treasure her friendship.

My husband, Peter Schroeder, helped Linda and I with the editing and reading of Tiers of Healing for Groups. He was instrumental in getting the Tiers of Healing Self Study Guides completed and is editing Tiers of Helping and Tiers of Hope. Peter is the miracle that God sent to me as answered prayer in 1988. He continues to inspire me, strengthen me, hold me and without him my life would be much less bright. I love you, Peter.

Finally, I must acknowledge my mentor, teacher and friend, Debbie Ford. Thank you, Debbie for your work, your guidance, your love.

TIERS OF HEALING
TIER I - A JOURNEY THROUGH GRIEF
Self Guided Workbook I

TABLE OF CONTENTS

SESSIONS . . . . PAGE

1. SELF-CARE CONTRACT 1

2. STAGES OF GRIEF 7

3. A PLACE OF PEACE 11

4. STUGS 13

5. ANGER 15

6. COMMUNICATING 19

7. RELATIONSHIPS 23

8. AKERU 27

9. YOU ARE NOT ALONE 31

10. ACKNOWLEDGE YOURSELF 35

TIERS OF HEALING I
SESSION 1
SELF-CARE CONTRACT

Nothing is worth more than this day.
You cannot relive yesterday.
Tomorrow is still beyond your reach.
—Johann Wolfgang Von Goethe

Music Suggestion: "Hero" by Mariah Carey

On the stress scale, death of a spouse is ranked No. 1 and divorce is No. 2; loss of health, job, and home are all in the top ten. Loss is stressful, and stress can be deadly. It is imperative to take special care of yourself as you move through your loss. Heart disease, stroke, cancer, and diabetes are rampant in our communities and are all closely linked to stress.

A recent European study indicates that breast cancer is prevalent among women who have been separated and divorced. Further studies show that within three years of becoming separated and/or divorced, many women become ill with stress-related diseases. Stress kills. Self-care is not an option—it is a necessity, especially during times of loss.

Your life has been turned upside down. Perhaps your living space has changed. Your family and friends have little knowledge of what to do with you or for you. Your workload may have doubled and your future dreams suddenly disappeared. You are in a time of tremendous change that you did not actively choose. To top it all off, you are most likely responsible for *all* the daily activities in your life. It is up to you to begin to take additional care of yourself. For some individuals, this could actually create stress, as it may be easier to care for others. If your tendency is to forget yourself and concentrate on others, remember the flight attendant's words: "Place the mask on your face *first* before helping another."

We believe in self-care so much that we put it right at the beginning of the program and have included it throughout the course. We urge you to find a buddy to hold you accountable for your self-care contract. We are serious and ask that you sign and date a self-care contract and keep your word to yourself.

Each of us has a powerful life force within us. The Chinese call it *Qi*; the Japanese call it *Ki*. In the yogic traditions of India and Tibet, the Ayurveda calls it *Prana*. The Jewish Kabalistic tradition refers to this energy as *yesod*. In the Christian faith, this life force is often referred to as the *Holy Spirit*. The Lakota tribes of the First People of North America call the energy *waka*, and the Iroquois tribe refers to this powerful force as *orenda*. In simple terms, it is the vital energy that fuels our bodies, minds, and spirits. What you call it is your choice. You only have to nurture it and it will grow stronger.

Physical well-being is inseparable from emotional well-being, and emotional well-being is inseparable from spiritual well-being. Each day, you have the opportunity to increase or decrease your state of well-being. Take a moment to think about what you do daily that impacts your vital life force. What do you do that depletes it? Who seems to drain you? What are your thoughts or beliefs that sap this energy? **List some of what takes away from your energy in your journal or pad of paper.**

Now write down what adds to your life force. Whom do you count on to help you smile, laugh, and feel good about the world? What thoughts make your heart sing or make you laugh out loud? What foods do you eat that give you an inner energy and peaceful spirit? Are there books you read, songs you listen to, places you visit that enliven you and lift your spirits? What tasks leave you feeling accomplished and fulfilled? List everything you can think of that contributes to your state of well-being. Depending on how long ago your loss was, you may not believe that anything can lift you or bring you a sense of peace. Please do this exercise despite your feelings. Perhaps just getting out of bed and brushing your teeth or actually eating a warm meal is all you can manage for now. Wherever you are able to start, you must start.

Grief and loss affect our bodies, minds, thoughts, and spirits. Imagine how you would care for yourself if you had a severe case of the flu. You would rest, eat healthy foods, get enough sleep, and avoid situations that worsened your symptoms. As you will see in the next session, grief has stages, and with proper care, these stages can be shortened. Poor eating habits, lack of sleep, drinking to excess, and lack of hygiene only exacerbate the symptoms of grief.

Please take the time now to fill out your Self-Care Contract. Be certain to include sleep, food, times of quiet and reflection, proper hygiene, and some type of movement (exercise, walking, dancing, gardening—choose what you love). You may want to print this contract and put it in a place you will see daily. Copy a few blank contracts and periodically increase your own self-care.

You are vitally important. Take good care of yourself.

SELF – CARE CONTRACT

I, _____, commit myself to the following self-care beginning this
week. List what you will actually do:

_____

_____

_____

_____

_____

_____

_____

_____

_____

_____

(Make sure this is a realistic and measurable plan.)

I will begin working on self-care on _____ for _____
                                            DATE   **LENGTH OF TIME**

When I reach this goal, I will reward myself with:

I will evaluate the achievement of this goal with my support person. (Be certain to find
someone to hold you accountable for this contract.)

Name: _____

Date: _____

How to contact: _____ (phone, e-mail, in person)

How often to contact: _____ (daily, weekly)

Signed: _____

Support person: _____ Date: _____

Exercises for Session 1:

1. Create a place for your "inner work." A place to listen to or read uplifting words. Be sure it is a place you enjoy and take pride in. This could be a separate room, a corner in a closet, or a special chair you feel safe in and bless with your thoughts.

2. Take five minutes a day to be in this special place and say the words "Today I will remember to honor myself at the deepest level. Today I will remember I am not alone."

3. Begin to track your moods, your spirit, and your day using the Weather Report Chart that follows. We have provided you with six months. Feel free to copy the form and continue through this first year to track your days. Name your day as if it were the weather. For example, a sunny day may mean you feel hopeful; stormy could mean your anger is up or that you feel like screaming and crying all day; rainy could mean tears or sadness. It is important to track how you are doing. Often, we are unaware of how much we have grown or how much we are sinking. Do this daily, and hopefully, you'll soon notice that there are more and more sunny days.

Weather Report Chart
Month/Year

Sun	Mon	Tues	Wed	Thu	Fri	Sat

TIERS OF HEALING I
SESSION 2
STAGES OF GRIEF

Don't be afraid that your life will end;
be afraid that it will never begin.
—Grace Hansen

Music Suggestion: "Welcome to Wherever You Are" by Bon Jovi

Do you believe there is a right way to grieve? Do you believe you must take certain steps, you must cry only a certain amount, or you must be up and active within a certain time frame? If you believe everyone grieves in the same way and there is a set, structured approach to grieving, you are wrong.

There is no "right way" to grieve. Grief is an emotion that is part of the human experience. Humans are not the only species to grieve. Elephants spend days clustered over a deceased member of their herd. Pets that may seem to be sworn enemies actually exhibit intense stress reactions when separated. Their symptoms may actually be identical to human grief, including sleep disorders, sighing, restlessness, and even depression.

Grief is a normal reaction to any significant loss. It is a natural process, and the only way to heal from grief is allowing the process; otherwise, it will flare up for years, even decades, down the road.

Although there may not be a "right way" to grieve, grief has been studied by numerous professionals. Perhaps the most famous study was conducted by Elizabeth Kubler-Ross. She did her groundbreaking work with terminally ill patients, but the stages of grief also apply to any life loss, whether real or perceived.

In this session, you will learn the different stages of grief. Please remember that these are not steps lined up in a nice, neat row. Each stage has its own continuum. At times, it may feel as though you are the ball in a pinball machine, bouncing from stage to stage and back again. You may feel bruised in the process. Remember, there is no right way to grieve.

Why is it important to know the different stages of grief? Knowing where you are assists you in moving to the next place. Imagine if you were driving and had no idea where you were, would you keep driving? Or would you stop to find out where you were and then determine where you wanted to go? It is helpful to know where you are going as you navigate this loss you are moving through.

It helps you to know what you are feeling is normal. It's a little like having the stomach flu. If you know it is flu, you know that what you are experiencing is normal. You know that you have not been poisoned. You know once the process is complete, you will feel better. Once the process of grief is complete, you will feel better.

The first stage of grief is **shock**. Facts do not sink in. You feel as if you are on a deadly roller coaster with no way off. Shock may be the way the universe shields us from what is horrific. Shock may last days or sometimes a few weeks.

The next stage is **denial**. Our psyches use this stage to avoid the inevitable. Things we say when we are in denial may sound something like, "I'm sure it is nothing," "He'll be back," "She can't be dead," or "They will call me back in a few weeks." Denial is manifested in other ways by refusing to do what must be done—sorting through clothing, paying bills, leaving a voice mail message on an answering machine, setting a place at the table for the departed, or avoiding doctor visits and tests. Denial takes many shapes and serves as a protective layer as we begin to accept the unacceptable.

As we continue on the roller coaster ride of grief, the next turn brings **anger**. Frustration flares. The unfairness of your loss makes you stomp your feet, kick the wall, scream at shopkeepers. Anger is normal and healthy when it has appropriate outlets. We devote an entire session to anger later in the program. At this stage, just know that it is normal to be angry. Hurtful anger will not help you; healthy anger can be used to move forward. If you feel stuck in this place of anger, please go to the session on anger at any time.

The fourth step or stage of grief is **bargaining**. You bargain with God: "Get me through this, and I will start tithing and go to temple/church/mass daily," or "Give me back my excellent health, and I will never swear again." You may try to bargain with a person who has left: "Come back. I will do anything you want." We even bargain with ourselves: "If I promise myself to never have dessert, I can hang on to all his old toys," or "If I get out of bed today, I will not need to cry." Bargains are normal, and they all have one thing in common: they do not work. At the end of the day, we are still left with our loss.

When **shock**, **denial**, **anger**, and **bargaining** do not work, along comes **depression**. Sometimes depression can actually be a gift, as it may be a prelude to acceptance. For many, depression can last far too long and must be addressed by a professional. If you feel depressed and have been in this state for more than a few weeks or the depression keeps you from your daily routine, it is vitally important that you seek professional help.

Once we have passed through the first five stages of grief, we can then begin to move toward **acceptance**. We are now beginning to accept where we are. We may not like where we are, but we are accepting this new place in which we find ourselves. Acceptance is what you are aiming for even as you scream, "I will never, ever accept that my child died." Best-selling author Debbie Ford believes pain is in our resistance to what is. Acceptance is not conceding that what happened was right, good, or just. Acceptance is nothing more than finding yourself in a place and noting where you have arrived. You may not want to stay in Gary, Indiana, but that is where the car stopped. You may be in shock that the car died. You can be as angry as you want and blame a faulty mechanic. You can even bargain: "Get me the heck out of here, and I will never drive again." You may become depressed that you are in Gary and no longer in San Diego on the beach, but until you finally accept where you are, you are unable to make the plans to get out and get moving.

The stages of grief are tricksters. You may wake up on Monday morning brimming with hope, knowing you have finally gotten to a place of acceptance, and by bedtime, or maybe sooner, you are in the depths of depression and anger again. Grief work is like riding a roller coaster. There are twists, turns, steep climbs, and plummeting lows. The ride will end. Grief will dissolve. There is hope.

Exercises for Session 2:

1. Draw a roller coaster on white paper with crayons. Imagine it is your roller coaster of grief. How big is it? How many dips and turns? Now draw where you are on this coaster. Are you in shock, denial, anger—where are you?

2. Some of us get stuck in a particular stage. It is as if the roller coaster has stopped and we are still stuck in some turn. What does it mean to be stuck? What does it mean to be moving slowly through a particular stage? You are the one to answer this question. Are you stuck? What type of professional help can you get?

3. Below are symptoms that may appear during the stages of grief, along with suggestions that may help alleviate or diminish these symptoms. Note any symptoms you are having, and take the needed action to lessen the impact.

   A. **Memory Trouble:** During times of shock or extreme change, you may forget mundane activities (such as turning off the stove), your address, or the name of your favorite café. This is normal. Drink a lot of water, write yourself notes, and be patient. The more stressed you become about forgetting, the more you will forget!

   B. **Emotional Ups and Downs:** Your emotions may range from ecstatic to fear to excitement to despair, all in one hour! You are in a place of stress and change. This is normal. Water is your friend; drink a lot of it. Take daily vitamins, and perhaps check with a dietician about adding stress vitamins. Exercise! Journal about what you feel. Share your emotions with trusted others. Keep a diary of feelings (the Weather Report Chart) so you can begin to notice patterns or improvement.

   C. **Loss of Balance:** This may sound bizarre, but during times of stress, you do not want to be climbing ladders. The first year one of us was dealing with a loss, she hit a bicycle messenger, scraped her car against a tree, twisted her ankle, and broke over a dozen glasses. Take care where you walk, how you drive, and **stay off ladders**.

   D. **Sleeping Problems:** No sleep, too much sleep, or waking up in the middle of the night are all normal. Drink water, avoid caffeine and large amounts of alcohol, eat starches for dinner, and leave protein for early in the day. Have a nice, safe ritual to say good night to your body and mind. Write or journal before going to sleep. If you wake up in the middle of the night, get up and do a chore you hate (one of us did the ironing), then go back to bed. Pretty soon you will not want to do the chore! Try to avoid sleep medications unless you have a doctor who is closely monitoring the dose and amount. Warm milk, a warm bath, and a not-so-great book can do wonders to aid in sleep.

   E. **High Sensitivity to Stress:** You are in a place of stress. Any additional stress can seem monumental. Give yourself a vacation from any activity you can safely avoid. Let go of holiday "have-tos." Only see those people who make you laugh or hold you while you cry. Shop when there are no crowds. Drink water, exercise, and spend time in your place of safety.

TIERS OF HEALING I
SESSION 3
A PLACE OF PEACE

There is a light that this world cannot give.
Yet you can give it, as it was given you.
And as you give it, it shines forth
To call you from the world and follow it.
For this light will attract you
As nothing in this world can do.
Ask for light
And learn that you are light.
—A Course in Miracles

Music Suggestion: "The Rose" by Bette Midler

As you move through the experience of grief, you may notice the ebb and flow of life has its ups and downs. The ups and downs will always be here. It is how you manage the ups and downs of life that determines your level of peace, not just within yourself, but within the world you live in. In *A Return to Love*, Marianne Williamson states that "the change we are looking for is really inside our heads." Changes are always going to happen; they're a part of being a human being. Many times, we are unable to change our outer circumstances. What we can change, however, is how we perceive these circumstances. That shift in perception is what Williamson calls a miracle.

Love resides within each one of us. Love is not produced by another being or situation. The situation or person we find ourselves with may tap into the love we were born with, but love always lives within us. We have the ability to tap into this love any time we choose.

As humans, it seems as if it is infinitely easier to love, nurture, and acknowledge *others* when they are in pain than to love, nurture, and acknowledge *ourselves* when we are in pain. If we listen to our thoughts during times of loss, we are likely to find ourselves beating ourselves up and feeling like victims. Turning these thoughts around and finding a place of peace within you is the start of a new way of being in the world. It is a way that will remain long after the grief dissolves.

Each of us will find this place of peace in a different way. Quiet is necessary, as is a place free of distractions. Close your eyes and focus your attention on your breath, which is deep and audible. If you have thoughts, just notice them, always bringing your attention back to your breath. As you breathe, allow your imagination to take over. Imagine a superhero part of yourself or your higher self. This part is the most loving, giving, peaceful being you have ever met. Imagine what this superhero might look like, how they are dressed, perhaps taking on the form of an angel or a saint. Fully imagine the part that is connected to the divine universe and what it may bring to you. Keep breathing and allow yourself to experience the wonder and gratitude you feel. If you have any emotion, allow it to surface, and stay connected to your place of peace. Tap your heart and acknowledge this is a part of you. It is always available. Always with you.

Exercises for Session 3:

Supplies needed: Crayons, paper or poster board, glue, magazines, and music

1. Practice connecting with your place of peace daily for three to five minutes. Notice if there is anything your superhero or higher self wants to share with you.

2. Create what your place of peace looks like. You may use white paper or poster board. Put the words MY PLACE OF PEACE at the top of the paper. Now put on your favorite peaceful music and draw or cut pictures from magazines and glue on the paper what represents your place of peace. Once complete, put your collage or drawing in a place in your home where you can imagine stepping into it (the place you created) once or twice a day for ten to fifteen seconds.

TIERS OF HEALING I
SESSION 4
STUGS

We all need both roots and wings, but our life may be a continuous struggle between our roots and our wings, our desire to stay put and be productive and grow, and our desire to dream of other possibilities and fly off to achieve that dream. In resolving that struggle we can become both more rooted and more free to move out. —Sister Stanislaus Kennedy, Gardening the Soul

Music Suggestion: "The Way We Were" by Barbara Streisand

It is important that you are completing the exercises at the end of each session and keeping your contract for self-care. Take a moment to review where you are at this moment. Where are you on the roller coaster of grief? Are you keeping your word to yourself in regard to self-care? Do you have your place of peace established, and are you dwelling there daily? This is your life and your healing—show up for yourself.

Sudden Temporary Upsurgences of Grief (STUGS) show up when you least expect them. Perhaps you are doing all the exercises, you are feeling a little bit better, your Weather Report shows a few sunny days every week, and then one day you hear a song, smell a familiar odor, or find a beloved's belonging in an unexpected place, and your insides crash. This is what we call STUGS. They are the sudden and surprising things that trigger our memories. They come with both positive and negative images that are imbedded in our psyches.

At times, STUGS may bring up fearful feelings or deep grief and sadness. They may appear on special days such as birthdays, anniversaries, the change of seasons, or holidays. At other times, the smell of a favorite food or perfume can trigger STUGS.

Please keep in mind that you are still making progress despite an upsurgence of unexpected grief. Your self-care plan is important, as much as your mentor, coach, or good friend is important. Sometimes sharing what happened and seeing it as a normal part of this process will help dissipate the strong feelings of grief that have reappeared. At other times, you may want to spend time in your place of peace or journal about what is happening and how you feel.

Be certain to do the exercises that follow. Remember when you were a child and you practiced fire drills? We have a type of fire drill for you to practice. Becoming prepared for those times when grief takes you by storm will help lessen the power and severity of the attack.

Exercises for Session 4

Supplies needed: Index cards

1. Make a list of possible situations that could trigger active grief. Include anything and anyone you think may put you back in a place of sudden grief. Examples we have seen and experienced are as follows: unpacking Christmas ornaments, the backs of men/women who dress and are similar to our loved one, seeing an ex-spouse at a shopping center, cars that remind you of what you lost, songs, pipe tobacco, movies, particular times of year, a blazing fire in a fireplace, smells of steaks cooking on the grill, the pop of champagne, children swinging, a baby blanket, advertisements for pregnant women, and so on. The list is endless, just as the types of loss are endless. Remember, pain is universal; misery is not.

2. Once you have a good long list (at least twenty-five items) pick the top five that could actually occur. Write that situation on the front of a three-by-five index card. For example, *My sister tells me she is pregnant.*

3. On the back of this same three-by-five card, write what positive action you will take to move out of the feeling of active grief. You can call a friend, say a prayer, tell yourself you are moving forward, or go for a walk. You may even write or take time to cry. Imagine what will help you the most in that situation. You always want to take a deep breath as you experience the situation, and then perform the action you listed. If you can't think of anything that will help, call a friend or email us.

4. You will now have five index cards with a situation on the front and a solution on the back. It is *very* important to practice and practice. Read the situation and immediately imagine performing the healing action. Do this *before* the situation presents itself. The secret of life is practice.

TIERS OF HEALING I
SESSION 5
ANGER

The more you have been weighed down by reminders of your inadequacies, the more inclined you will be to harbor anger. Disempowering thoughts lower our self-esteem and may impede the road to healing. We differ in the ways we allow our anger to express itself. In some cases, suppressed anger turns into depression, or apathy sets in. Some may develop a cynical edge that prompts adversarial or sarcastic remarks.
—Linda DeBelser

Music Suggestion: Any good rock song—play it loud!

Anger is a necessary part of the grief process when we are going through a time of loss and healing. This is not the time to continue to hide the buried feelings of the past, but rather a time to release and heal them. As human beings experience a significant loss, other losses from the past that were not dealt with at the time can cascade into the feelings of today. Grief must be worked through. It does not go away; it is only delayed. Anger not expressed becomes toxic and may erupt in an out-of-control rage or begin to turn inward, shutting down your life force. Anger expressed in a healthy and safe way can actually benefit you.

Research tells us that the average person tends to remain angry for about three years after an actual loss! That type of anger is not healthy or beneficial and can only serve to attack the cells of the body and spirit.

The first step in overcoming anger is accepting and recognizing our anger for what it is and then beginning to heal our wounded selves.

The second step is looking inside ourselves to find the wounded parts and then beginning to explore the causes of our individual anger.

The third step is developing a strategy for dealing with anger. Most often, if we are willing to look deep enough, we discover we are angriest with ourselves. Before we can forgive, it is necessary to acknowledge the anger involved. We will also address anger in Tier 2, as it is an ongoing part of the healing process.

There are two basic timelines for anger: present and past. Present anger pertains to anger that occurs and is expressed over a recent situation or experience. Past anger is anger that is inappropriately displayed in the present because of something that happened in the past. In addition to the different timelines of anger, there are also different styles of anger:

- **Anger Avoidance:** People who have this particular style shy away from anger. They are afraid of their own and others' anger. They may be afraid of the power of their anger. They see themselves as "nice" because they do not show anger. These individuals often do not recognize when it is important to be angry and therefore lose some of their healthy survival skills. In other words, they can become doormats and allow others to walk all over them.

- **Sneaky Anger:** These individuals never let anyone know they are angry. They may become passive aggressive. When angry, they may forget things, not follow through on plans, and say "Yeah, but…" quite often. By doing little or nothing and communicating nothing about their plans, they frustrate their families and thwart others' plans. These people often don't know what they want in their own lives.

- **Paranoid Anger:** These people feel others are out to get them and take away what is theirs. They tend to project their anger on others. They see everyone else as angry, but do not own their own anger. Their anger is disguised as self-protection, and they are defensive of their families and possessions. Paranoids are by definition untrusting and also insecure.

- **Sudden Anger:** Think of a volcano and you will know what type of anger these individuals express. They erupt out of the blue, spew their venom everywhere, and leave. Often, they leave a trail of destruction that can take a long time to repair. They give themselves permission to "blow" so they are able to feel good about themselves. People who use this type of anger gain an instant surge of power, but they can also be dangerous to themselves and others. They say and do things they often regret, but by then, the damage has been done and it is too late to undo the eruption.

- **Shame-Based Anger:** If you are super-sensitive and tend to take everything personally, you may want to explore any deep-seated shame that you may be carrying. People with this type of anger often end up attacking the people they love, which then makes them feel even more shame.

- **Deliberate Anger:** These people use anger to control others. They get what they want by threatening and overpowering others. This style eventually backfires when others leave or plan revenge.

- **Addictive Anger:** Some people get an anger rush and emotional high from anger. They enjoy the intensity and emotional power they get when they explode, as this type of style typically is explosive. They will actually pick fights and often end up entangled with the law.

- **Habitual Anger.** A close cousin to the addictive style, habitual anger begins to run (and ruin) the lives of all involved. These people are always angry. They rarely have close friends, as people avoid them and their constant, never-ending anger.

- **Moral Anger:** These people are the judge and the jury. They decide who and what is right and wrong. They are on the attack and believe their anger is justified. They have one way to deal with differences: anger.

- **Hate:** Taking anger one step forward, people turn anger into hatred. The hater vows to despise the offender, and forgiveness (where healing will eventually take place) is not an option. Hatred is a poison that hurts the world.

What is your style? What do you recognize about your anger from the preceding list? Is there another style? Is there healthy anger? Yes. Please do the exercises that follow and begin to develop healthy styles of anger expression.

Exercises for Session 5

1. Make a list of current and past angers. Even if you believe you are not angry, make the list.

2. Choose one person on the list and write a letter of anger to this person. Use "I" language, taking responsibility for your anger (e.g., *Dear ___, I am so angry when I recall all the times I urged you to go to the doctor. I asked you several times to make an appointment and get a checkup. You could be alive today if you had known you had a weak heart. I am furious.*) Do not mail the letter. You may keep it, tear it into small pieces, or burn it.

3. When you feel anger welling up inside of you:

    A. Take a deep breath. Use your breath to calm yourself and relax your muscles.

    B. Count to ten (this actually works). Talk to yourself. Make a decision about whether this is something you want or need to be angry about. Breathe.

    C. Ask yourself if this is something that needs to be worked out with another person or handled internally.

    D. Express your anger in a calm manner. Be specific about the cause of your anger, using "I" sentences and owning your own anger (e.g., *I feel so angry when you forget that we have plans. I am under stress right now, and when you do not call and forget that we made a date, I feel deserted and I am furious.*).

    E. Avoid name-calling, sarcasm, put-downs, judgments, criticism, and by no means ever begin a physical attack.

    F. If you feel as though you will "blow" or fly off the handle, remove yourself from the situation, take a walk, do some form of physical release that is not harmful (hit a punching bag, throwing bags of ice against a brick wall, batting a pillow with a plastic bat, going for a run, etc.). Once the anger surge is released, you may go back to the individual and express your anger in a calm manner (see the fourth point above).

    G. Stay in the present and do not bring up things from the past. If you have past anger, schedule a time to express that anger.

    H. Own your anger and work toward a possible solution.

    I. Write your anger out in a letter, but do not send it. Tear it up and write another letter. Tear that one up as well—until you are able to calmly express your anger and ask for what you want.

    J. Thich Nhat Hanh, the revered Vietnamese monk, advises us to water the seeds of joy rather than the seeds of anger. Eventually, you will find so many things to be grateful for and joyful about that you will no longer need to vent your anger.

    K. Pray for the person with whom you are angry. This is difficult, but it works. Say, "I pray for ____. I am sorry for any part I may have played in this situation that has caused me such anger (you do not need to know what you did to say this prayer), and I release any anger I may have."

L. If your anger is taking on a life of its own, if you find yourself raging at or hurting others, you *must* seek professional help. The consequences of this type of anger are long lasting and filled with hurt and regret.

TIERS OF HEALING I
SESSION 6
COMMUNICATION

Use your words as weapons and you wound yourself as well as others. Use your words with love and you encourage the love of others as well as the love of yourself.
—Linda DeBelser

Music Suggestion: "Happy Talk" by South Pacific

Communicating is an art form. Communication can be difficult during the best of times, but during times of loss, chaos, and change, communication can become a major stumbling block in your healing process.

During times of healing from loss, it is extremely important to pay attention to the way you communicate. This is a time to be gentle with yourself. How you ensure safety in your communication is up to you to decide. If children are present and affected by a loss, they must be a primary consideration in how you communicate.

The first place to begin is with your self-talk. You absolutely must talk positively to yourself. Use deep breathing to calm and center yourself. Rephrase the words you say to yourself to assure they are positive. Remember, healing requires patience and gentleness.

Watch the words you say to others, especially children. Be careful of words such as *always*, *never*, and *forever*, as they leave little or no room for change. Using dramatic words such as *nightmare*, *terrible*, or *horrible* as well as phrases like, "I want to die" or "I hate my life" paint a picture of negativity and hopelessness. You may truly wish you were in some other life, and there may be days when you feel as if you are trapped in a nightmare. However, those are just days, just moments, and they won't last forever. You are here because your spirit has something to finish, something to accomplish. There is hope. Use words that reflect that hope. In the 12 Step Traditions, there is the phrase "Fake it till you make it." Sometimes we are asked to act "as if." You may not be able to act as if your life is perfectly on track, but you can use positive words to plant the seeds of what your life is becoming.

During times of loss, communication styles need to change. Small talk, such as listening to a friend who has the latest gossip, may have been great in the past, but now may leave you feeling empty or irritated. Let friends know how you have changed. You may say to them, "Instead of hearing about the movie you saw, I would like to hear about what is the important to you today." To the gossipmonger, a simple statement of "After the death of ___, I swore off gossiping. Would you help me stick to my resolve?" may work wonders. True friends will honor your wishes.

Roles also change during great loss. Those who were the caretakers of the family and the community may now find they are barely able to care for themselves. This is the time to set firm boundaries and say no. "Thank you, I am unable to do that right now" is all that needs to be said. You need not explain. This is not rude; this is assertive self-care.

Remember to use "I" phrasing, as discussed in the session on anger. Often, friends, acquaintances, and family members have no idea how to help you. They would be pleased to have you ask them for help in a specific way. Tell others what would help you the most. Examples we have used are as follows:

- "I could use someone to just come in and read the kids a story. I have not been able to read them a story since ___ left."
- "What I need the most right now is someone to just listen. I know that no one can fix this, but I just want to tell someone my good memories."
- "I need a handyman, accountant, attorney, cleaning service, dog sitter, etc. Would you make some calls and find me one?"

Be specific in your requests.

Be firm in letting others know you are not up to company, baking cookies, going to nightclubs, or hosting the local dance troupe. If there are those who ask you, "When are you going to get over this?" let them know you are not certain when that time will be, and it would be helpful if they did not ask that type of question. People who have suffered a loss know it takes a long time. The first year is the most difficult because it has all of the "firsts": first holiday, first back-to-school day, first day of pool season, first birthday, first anniversary, and so on. It is a long list, and those individuals who ask when you will stop crying and be "back to normal" need to be told you will never be "back to normal." You are moving forward to a new normal, and you have no idea of how that will look. Sometimes you must ask certain people to stop calling you. These may be longtime friends who do not listen to what you need and do not respect the boundaries you have set. Stop returning their calls, and if need be, sit them down, look them in the eye, and tell them, "I am unable to talk to you while I am healing. I have asked you to refrain from negative talk about ___ when the children are around, and yet you continue. I have asked you to please let me be sad, and you insist on telling me why it is good that he/she left. Right now, while I am fighting to find hope and a new tomorrow, I cannot talk with you." Hold your ground.

As we said in the anger session, it is perfectly OK to write an angry e-mail, letter, or text. **Do not send it.** Wait a week and work through your anger. Use other ways to express your anger. Another type of letter, e-mail, or text that we urge you not to send is of the "please come home, please come back, I will do anything" variety. These types of correspondence will leave you feeling ashamed at a later date. "Write it, but don't send it" is a good rule for the first year of moving through a loss. If you have a trusted coach, mentor, minister, or even therapist, show him or her the letter you would like to send before you say something you cannot take back.

If your loss is a divorce, you may be tempted to involve your children in communicating with your ex-spouse or soon-to-be ex. **You must never do this.** In addition to bad-mouthing your ex, confiding your hurt in your children puts them in a terrible position. Children need two parents. You may believe your ex is unable to parent or is a danger to your children. Take this to your attorney, not to your children. As coaches and counselors, we have sat with thousands of people who are still working through the trauma of their parents' divorce from decades ago. Your children are children, even if they are grown. You are the adult.

Communicating is a lifelong skill to continually improve upon. You may use this time of healing to have meaningful, honest, specific dialogue. It will serve you in the future.

Exercises for Session 6

1. Erase the words *should, have to, always,* and *never* from your vocabulary. Replace these terms with *could, choose to, sometimes,* and *right now.* Notice the shift in how you feel when you choose a different word.

2. For one week, when you are asked to do something, respond with, "May I get back to you on that?" Allow yourself at least twelve to twenty-four hours or longer to decide what will best serve you in your healing journey. Say no unless you know it will help your healing.

3. If you find yourself on an unpleasant call, let the person on the other end know you must hang up right now. Then hang up the phone.

4. If you are dealing with children's questions about why, let them know you do not know. In fact, you'd like to know why as well. Reassure them that they (and you) will be OK and that you love them. Family counseling with a minister or professional therapist may help. Ask for what you need for yourself and your children.

Each relationship you have with another person reflects
the relationship you have with yourself. —Alice DeVille

Music Suggestion: "The Story of My Life" by Neil Diamond

The most important relationships we have are those with the universe and ourselves. How do you see yourself in the world? Are you a small child needing protection, an independent "I can do it myself, I don't need help" type, or a damsel in distress waiting for a white knight to save you? What type of relationship do you want to have with the world and yourself? If what you want is more self-trust, self-respect, or spontaneity, this is a good time to begin the process.

Healthy people have healthy relationships. Notice where you have been in the past and what steps you could take to shift the types of relationships that do not work for you. Decide now that a part of your healing journey will include fostering healthy relationships for yourself now and in the future. Below are several types of relationship styles Virginia Satir, noted family therapist, described:

- **The A-Frame Dependency Relationship:** Two people lean on each other because they have not learned to be whole. If one person leaves this A-frame, the other falls. If one decides to grow, it is difficult to step away and create a healthy give-and-take.

- **The Pedestal Relationship:** One person is placed on a pedestal and the other worships them. The person doing the worshipping has an idealized image of the other and becomes angry, disappointed, and demanding if the one on the pedestal falls short. The person on the pedestal is unable to share their innermost feelings and desires, as they must be in a place of adoration, not love.

- **The Smothering Relationship:** This is often seen in first-love relationships. The couple is attached at the hip and unable to move or go anywhere alone. This relationship has little room for growth and frequently sounds like, "I cannot live without you. I will devote myself to being with only you forever. I only need you to be happy." Often, this relationship feels exciting and intense in the beginning, but eventually, one or the other feels trapped, smothered, or unable to breathe.

- **The Master-Slave Relationship:** This type of relationship is often characterized by the words "I am the head of this house; what I say goes. I am the boss, and there will be no discussion. We will do it my way because I know best." The master can be female or male. In many relationships, one person is stronger or has a more powerful personality than the other. This may work for a while. The danger is this can become rigid and inflexible, and often, there is a great deal of emotional distance. Quite often, it is actually an insecure person who sets themselves up as master in order to control their surroundings.

- **The Boardinghouse Relationship:** This relationship involves little, if any, communication. Time spent together typically involves watching TV while eating and going in separate directions the rest of the time. This can be a confining relationship with two individuals growing apart and not even knowing that their relationship is suffering.

- **The Martyr Relationship:** The martyr, though sometimes pitied, is actually a very controlling person. This person typically controls through guilt. The people involved with a martyr often find it difficult to express feelings of anger or disagreement, as they feel guilty for all the martyr has sacrificed.

- **The Healthy Love Relationship:** The healthy love relationship involves two people who are whole. They have no need to control the other or be worshipped. They respect each other's space and trust they will be helped and supported when necessary. They are able to walk hand in hand as equals, choosing to be together.

How do you form healthy relationships? Begin to notice the types of relationships you have had or are having. Be honest with yourself. Determine that, going forward, as you become whole and healthy, you will attract those people into your life who are whole and healthy.

Exercises for Session 7

1. Make a drawing representing the types of relationship you have had in the past. Use stick figures. As you look at these pictures, ask yourself, "What could I do differently to change how I relate?" Draw your response.

2. Write a one-page story of what a healthy relationship looks like to you. Find role models from fiction, history, or people you know, and begin to analyze what they do to have successful, healthy relationships.

3. Take a class in relationship building. Look online or through your local park district or community college. There are numerous books devoted to healthy relationships. Remember, all relationship can be healthy.

One day, leafing through a Japanese dictionary, I came upon a word that caused me to marvel because it had so many different meanings—and all of them pertained to abandonment. The word is ak̲e̲ru. *It means "to pierce, to open, to end, to make a hole in, to start, to expire, to unwrap, to turn over." When someone leaves,* ak̲e̲ru *refers to the empty space that is created, the opening in which a new beginning can take place. I was amazed at the power of a single word that could suggest that to begin and to end are the same part of one never-ending cycle of renewal and healing.*
—Anne Browning

Music Suggestion: "How Could Anyone" by Shaina Noll

No matter the loss, the majority of individuals experiencing a significant loss—illness, job loss, death of a loved one, divorce, or loss of home and finances—all experience a sense of abandonment. Perhaps it is society that has abandoned them, friends, government, their church, or community. It may not even be a factual abandonment, but a person experiencing a loss *feels* abandoned. This is a normal feeling, and much like the stages of grief, the stages of *akeru* are not neat nor predictable. What they are is normal.

Often, feelings of a current abandonment trigger old childhood wounds, bringing up feelings of fear, insecurity, and self-doubt. You may feel desperate and powerless and believe you have lost your whole life. Anxiety may appear, along with the sense that you have no one to turn to.

Below are the five stages of *akeru*:

1. **Shattering:** Shattering can be unique to each individual. Some may feel totally bereft, while others manage to cope fairly normally, and still others may appear to move as if nothing major has happened. Each journey is different. What is important is to know your path. The pain of shattering physically can feel as if your heart is actually shattering or breaking. Science is just beginning to understand that our emotions affect us at a cellular level. When we say that we have heartache, we may actually feel as if our chests were hit with a baseball bat or that we are being ripped apart. Anxiety attacks may be common at this stage, as are suicidal thoughts. **You must immediately contact your physician or a professional health worker if you experience suicidal thoughts. There is help and hope.** During this stage, whether we like it or not, we are beginning to discover there is no knight in shining armor coming to our rescue. We are beginning to realize we are solely responsible for ourselves. This thought alone can be terrifying. It is important to seek out the love of family and friends at this time. A simple movie or time spent shopping can sometimes assure you that you are not alone. Be certain you are following your Self-Care Contract daily. This is also a good time to get a healing massage or even a pedicure.

2. **Withdrawal:** Withdrawal can be the most painful part of this journey. Withdrawing from reality means you fantasize about having your old life back. This is normal and similar to denial in the

stages of grief we discussed earlier. This fantasy keeps you from moving forward to the new life that awaits you. Remind yourself that you have no idea what your new life may look like or how you will feel in the future. You may be prepared to beg, bargain, and do almost anything to get your former life back; you may feel you would sell your soul to feel better. During this stage, it is very important that you do not make major decisions or become involved in legal settlements. If life dictates that you must sign contracts or make large decisions, find a trusted attorney or professional who can offer an unbiased opinion. This stage is similar to drug withdrawal. It is an addiction to the familiar past that keeps you stuck and unable to move forward. Withdrawal is the most vulnerable stage of healing. Seek the help of friends, family, therapists, and group programs (such as Tiers of Healing). Withdrawal is where you will do your soul-searching and eventually be led back to the uniqueness of you.

3. **Internalizing:** This is often the stage where the individual internalizes their rage. If you are experiencing this stage, you may be beating yourself up, blaming yourself, hating yourself, and dredging up all of your old mistakes and regrets. This is the time to clean up the wounds of the past and heal them. Whatever has happened has happened; it is impossible to go back in time. Forgive yourself and move forward as you learn from the past. Anger turned inward often leads to depression. Find a mentor or trusted friend to assist you with this difficult process. You could make a list of all you believe yourself responsible for—old mistakes and old losses—and make amends for anything that is possible to correct. For example, write letters of apology, pay back unsettled loans or stolen money, arrange to donate a gift in the person's name you believe you have wronged, etc. Once you have completed those tasks, write yourself a letter of forgiveness (e.g., *Dear Anne, I forgive you for your inability to save Rebecca's life. There are things that are out of your control, and I forgive you for not knowing what to do.*) If you find your rage is out of control, seek professional help immediately.

4. **Anger:** This is the fight-or-flight stage of separation and loss. As mentioned in the stages of grief and also the session on anger, this is normal and must be dealt with in a safe and productive way. Anger has the ability to be used to propel you and perhaps to use your loss as momentum to create lasting change. Some people have started foundations, began a movement (such as Mothers Against Drunk Driving), or changed laws as a result of their loss. They were fueled by the passion and force of their anger that others would not need to suffer the loss they experienced.

5. **Hope:** Hope is the beginning of the next level of your evolution. You are beginning to see the possibility that awaits you in the future. You are moving toward acceptance and are able to talk about your loss in a more detached manner. You can actually see a light at the end of this dark cave you have been moving through. Sometimes, when hope appears, it can induce feelings of guilt. You feel as if you are betraying the loss of a loved one, or you may believe if you move on, you will forget this dear loved one. You will never forget a loved one. They are in your heart and will move forward with you to what will become your new normal. Hope is a gift, and you have earned it. Relish in the hope of a new tomorrow.

Notice where you are in this process and what steps you can take at each stage to further your healing.

Exercises for Session 8

1. Identify the stage you are in during this time of *akeru*. Take out your Self-Care Contract and add new activities. Perhaps it is joining a support group or taking a class; maybe it is getting back to the basics of good eating and impeccable hygiene. Take your time as you determine what you can add to your self-care routine.

2. If you have children who are also suffering a loss, you may want to have them draw pictures of what they are experiencing, what they could do to help themselves, or what they need to feel safe and loved. Often, when a parent suffers a loss, the children suffer a double loss: the specific loss (death, divorce, finances, etc.) and the loss of the parent who is grieving. Get help for your children. This could be a young friend who takes them for a game day or a loving grandparent who can hold them. Do not believe your children are bouncing back. Children internalize loss and typically make very strong beliefs about themselves in regard to that loss. If you are unable to parent as you once did, get help.

TIERS OF HEALING I
SESSION 9
YOU ARE NOT ALONE

Somebody loves you more than you know.
Somebody goes with you wherever you go.
Somebody really and truly cares.
And lovingly listens to all of your prayers.
Don't doubt for a minute that this is true,
For God loves His children and takes care of them, too.
And all of His treasures are yours to share.
If you love Him completely and show Him you care.
And if you walk in His footsteps and have faith to believe,
There's nothing you ask for that you will not receive!
—Helen Steiner Rice, Daily Reflections

Music Suggestion: "I Know Who Holds Tomorrow" by Leanne Rimes

The subject of God during a time of grieving can bring up almost as many feelings as the initial loss. Many, many people will blame God for what they have lost; they are angry with God. Others may not believe in God and instead look to a higher power or universal spirit. Some individuals were brought up to believe that God is a punishing taskmaster and that God is punishing them for some misdeed. Whatever you believe is what you believe. This session is not concerned with your belief about the existence or non-existence of God. Rather, this session is designed to help you connect with an internal source or presence.

Higher Power, Mohammad, Buddha, Energy, The Great Spirit, Universal Knowledge, Creator, Mother God, Allah, or Jesus—whatever you call this being, this energy, science is beginning to give credence to something that connects the universe. The Unified Theory is fascinating, and much of it sounds like the ancients of old. We call this connection, this "stuff," God. As you read through this session, please replace the word you choose as we use the word *God*.

In the suggested music selection, Leanne Rimes sings about knowing who holds her hand. Oprah often talks about what she calls "God whispers." Some people refer to a "knowing" as a strange feeling, gut reaction, or instinct. Whatever these are for you, there have been instances in your life that took you by surprise, gave you a feeling of seeing a much larger picture, of perhaps getting a glimpse or feeling of tremendous love or peace. This may have happened recently or at some long-ago place in your childhood. Allow yourself to recall that feeling. It is a universal feeling, and human beings have been writing about it, singing about it, speaking about it, and sadly, going to war about it for millennia.

You may belong to a church, temple, or mosque or gather within a spiritual group. Or you may never have any type of spiritual experience. It is important that you begin to build trust and faith, in yourself, in your higher power. Whether you know it or not, you are being guided. The question is, are you listening?

When we are in pain, we are blind and deaf to all the gifts the universe has to offer. We may be busy blaming everyone and everything, including ourselves, for our present circumstances and not looking at what brings us joy, peace, love, and hope. The pain we are feeling is the pain of separation from the spirit within, the separation of heart and soul. Once we have the courage to look for meaning in our loss, we can begin to look for the resources to heal our wounded hearts. Mindful meditations, quiet space, journaling, and uplifting music are all ways to quiet the pain and connect with your heart and spirit. Stepping through your fear, having the courage to ask God for help, and being willing to hear the answers are just a few steps that will help you move forward on your journey to peace and wholeness.

In "The Voice for Love," David Paul and Candace Doyle tell us that the voice within us is a part of us. It is within the fabric of our being. Since we cannot separate from God, neither can this voice, and this voice is now a part of our mind. It is a part of our higher self that is always available to us and that can always lead us back to our oneness, to the state of peace and joy that we are. This voice is always there; we are never alone. It is there to guide us back to our understanding and our experience of the oneness we all share.

The qualities that come from this voice of God within us are love, compassion, joy, truth, honesty, kindness, hope, possibility, and the never-ending abundance of the universe. The voice of our ego or human fear speaks to resentment, anxiety, bitterness, judgment, and lack.

In her best-selling book, *The Right Questions*, Debbie Ford poses the question "Are we listening to our fear or our faith?" As I did the exercise on fear and faith, I called forth fear in my imagination, and I called forth faith in my imagination. In this imaginative meditation, I could hear the loud voice of fear telling me that I would be alone, I would never have what I longed for, and nothing would ever work out. In my meditation, I looked for the source of this loud voice and saw a small ant with a large megaphone (much like the wizard in *The Wizard of Oz*). That little ant was shouting for all he was worth. I then began to hear loud footsteps, and as I looked around, I discovered a huge giant. I could barely see his knees; this was faith. I could hear him whisper his name. "Why do you whisper?" I asked. "You are huge and could get my attention effortlessly." He softly said, "Fear is loud, but it is insignificant. Faith is quiet, but it can conquer all." I will never forget that amazing meditation, and I remember it anytime I feel afraid, alone, or desolate.

Faith can move mountains; fear would have us believe the mountain will crush us. In 12 Step groups, fear is sometimes described as "**F**alse **E**vidence **A**ppearing **R**eal." Your inner fear may be telling you that you are alone, that your life will never be good again, that you have failed, and that you have no more chances. This is a lie. Disregard it and find your true voice.

Exercises for Session 9

1. If you have not yet set up a place of peace in your home, do so now. It could be a small table or designated space on a dresser that acts as place of holiness, a type of altar. Place a candle, menorah, cross, picture, or holy book in this space. Use items that have meaning for you, items that connect you to the higher place within.

2. Write a prayer to place on your altar. It can be something simple or lengthy, more important is that it moves you, connects you. If you do not want to write your own prayer, find a poem or prayer that lifts your spirits, and place it where you can see it daily and recite it aloud each day.

3. Meditate (meditation can consist of simply breathing and quieting your thoughts) each day, and practice listening to the voice of inner wisdom that resides within you. If you do not hear or feel it, keep asking. It is a practice, and eventually, you will experience this voice. Journal about your experience.

4. Make a list of people who increase your faith. Surround yourself with these people.

5. Make a list of individuals who increase your fear or doubt. Avoid these people.

6. What evidence that appears real to you could actually be false? Make this question a part of your life.

TIERS OF HEALING I
SESSION 10
ACKNOWLEDGE YOURSELF

I read and walked for miles at night along the beach, writing bad blank verse and searching endlessly for someone wonderful who would step out of the darkness and change my life. It never crossed my mind that that person could be me. —Anna Quindlan

Music Suggestion: "One Moment in Time" by Whitney Houston

Taking time to acknowledge yourself is an important part of self-care. Self-acknowledgment is not bragging; it is recognizing the accomplishments you have made. Self-acknowledgment gives you the opportunity to note the hard work you have done and the barriers you have overcome. It feeds your resolve and lifts your spirit. Self-acknowledgment is not a luxury, but a necessity, especially during the long days of healing.

As you begin this process, be careful you do not compare yourself to others. Each of us is unique, and we each have our own piece to contribute and heal. Focus on yourself as you acknowledge your character, struggles, personal accomplishments, and willingness to work through the pain.

Within each of us are gifts that no one else has. Each of us has accomplished things that have improved our lives or the lives of others. Acknowledging yourself is not about memories or reminiscing. It is about claiming what you know to be true about yourself and smiling as you claim it.

During times of loss and healing, it is very important to take time regularly (we suggest daily) to acknowledge what you have done. There may be some days when the only thing on your list is "brushed teeth." The point is that you did it; you broke through a feeling, a thought, or a painful time and took action. **Acknowledge yourself.**

Many people, perhaps most, spend hours every day in negative self-talk. They berate themselves for what they did not do, what they forgot, or what poor choice they made. They then beat themselves up for having so much negative self-talk. If this sounds unproductive, it is. Vow now that you will acknowledge what steps you are taking, learn from steps you did not take, and continue to improve. Life is all about practice. Keep practicing. Keep acknowledging!

Exercises for Session 10

1. Find, purchase, or make yourself a beautiful box to hold your acknowledgments.

2. Begin to collect mementos you have saved that speak to you of some action you took, some time when you liked who you were. This could be a photo, an award certificate, a Boy or Girl Scout badge. Put these precious objects in your box, and as you do, say, "I acknowledge myself for____. I am an awesome human being."

3. Each day for twenty-eight days, write down ten things you did that contributed to your well-being. Every day, look for ten different things. We promise if you look, you will find them. Acknowledge yourself for your efforts, even if it was simply getting out of bed when all you wanted was to pull the covers over your head.

4. We at Tiers of Healing would love to hear about what you are doing to acknowledge yourself. Send us a list at anne@tiersofhealing.com or linda@tiersofhealing.com. We acknowledge your courage for taking this step.

Thank you for taking this Journey Through Grief. You have taken the first steps in finding hope and turning today's pain into tomorrow's joys. We are your number one fans and welcome your questions and feedback. If you are interested in finding out more about *Tiers of Healing*, please let us know. This journey, taken alone, can be powerful, and we believe when two or more gather to heal there is tremendous power. Forming communities is our particular passion. We welcome your input.

If you have purchased the set of books in the *Tiers of Healing* program, please begin Tier 2 when you feel ready. If you want to review Tier 1 and do the exercises again, you certainly may. As Peter Schroeder wrote, "It's Your Movie."

We honor you, we send you our love, and we know you can move through your loss and pain to reach a place of a new vision and a new reality. We are certain of your success.

In deep acknowledgment,
Anne Browning
Your fellow traveler

www.ingramcontent.com/pod-product-compliance
Lightning Source LLC
Chambersburg PA
CBHW081528040426

42447CB00013B/3375